blush / river / fox

multiverse

Series Editor
Chris Martin

Cover Description

The cover features a drawing by Anna Nygren made with red marker over a background of flat pale pink color. The drawing is of an amorphous four-footed imaginary creature with the face of a human wearing a quizzical expression and gazing out of the left side of the composition. The title appears in thick white lowercase serif type above the creature, and the author's name appears in thick magenta lowercase serif type at the bottom left, below the creature's two front feet.

blush / river / fox

anna nygren

MILKWEED EDITIONS

Milkweed Editions, 1011 Washington Avenue South, Suite 300,
Minneapolis, Minnesota 55415.
(800) 520-6455
milkweed.org

Published 2026 by Milkweed Editions
Printed in the United States of America
Cover design by Mary Austin Speaker
Cover art by Anna Nygren
Author photo by Louise Halvardsson
26 27 28 29 30   5 4 3 2 1
First Edition

Library of Congress Cataloging-in-Publication Data has been applied for.
LCCN: 2025026225.

for my family

Contents

blush / river / fox

blush

powder on pink wounds

skin in lips
lips in skin
mouth in hair
metal rails on weak
hair

the loops of the eye
soft inside
whisper
soft inside
eat as glazed
leave traces

oh mucus over concrete
the snail eat the snails
the plants grow
on the girl bodies
lay thrown of
them selves
in the hay
the hay the flesh
purple pink cheeks
under the eyes
meet all tender

an opening in to the head
the brain tumours
the outside of the inside
in to the inside
in to the within
a fold of head
a week of
relapse
falling forward over
rose leaf like the skin
bear like
give like
vitreous eye

the eye in the mouth
dragging over the skin
the room in the head
the hurting in the wound
cover with a blanket
tender to keep
look of mine
dream sequence
late to come
in over
soft skin
soft bones
skeleton that
the foxes and the dogs
leave nothing behind

thin dead lights
to never come over the lips
the mouth is a skin
wish in to the eye
let it see in the mouth
let it taste
calm rain
purple of everything

a pocket of skin and time
the pores are the holes
close to the heart
in to
inside
the flaps that open
the chambers
with the fingers through the hair
soft delicious
soft and care
breath   in
what has been bought for
christmas money
the last birthday
the last day
lay it close
feed it

tenderness mutilated
gross
whisper
gross
whisper tender
the tongue is the skin
the hair in the pores
the fat to bite
the metal in the skin
the teeth sticky
the fluid in the wounds
lick
a pocket of the skin

L I C K

pink brown red pink brown red pink brown red
forgive it in the s-
oul

the mother who drinks
tepid
lemon water
the bitter over the palate spray it
in the eyes
i split the forehead
against the plexi-
glass table
on the second floor
to lat-
er
fall down the stairs

so will the girl come
in to
me
so will she be dreamed
judged
drowned by lemon
soft and fluffy
extra softeners
like a lime-tree
meadow
dream of my surprise

so will the mother bear the leaves
the book open in her arms
the cat inside
the hair as the fur
assist
consist
lose
gasp
as
if
as
hiccup
hiccuping coughing snorting gasping slowly dampen drinking
falling full over the edge
miss the forehead
slints
the wounds

evil nylon
moist over the cold
hand under
hide rinse

white

pink

beige

powderbrown

bronze

The breath in the face
All
Ashes of a
Alms for girl
Watch
The breathing wholes
Weak spines
Alternativ
All

snow d r o p s
b u t t e r blooms
my soul

steal and hide
run and forget
wind still under the eyes
the laughter of the fools
place p l a c e
an island of
p l a s t i c
an I
would

“”

body of opening
leave it to
numb

glow

» can you puke out your heart «
» thanks «

the shame taste

I PROMISE NOT TO BE STUPID.

(her grief)

nice
things

omg

so. Alone. never. been.
toxic

LOO
K

do you think i dress
for you
do you think i lick
do you think

i
i
i
am u

little girl
seaking
the same

ehhhhhhhhhh

THE NIGHT

(blowout)

you destroy me whole

the hole

the hole

xoxo

the value of the smoke

likes

pizza

a row of backs
back
row
spine
i am this ugly girl can they stoppp shout can they come to
me come to me away from come come tear it out of the chest
a burning ball let it burn let it burn the light that throws up
on the pistasssscchhhe shoes does this concern no fold your
legs under bite with the bracelet in the skin until it bleads
out of the holes the whole head leave slowly alone stalker
seaking like play a little be too much lying
down
this
flow

wild animals

1.
You
You
You
You
You

2.
The white horses that
come in the summer for
summer
pasturage
we rush to look
you come
before
The white horses

3.
One is albino with
weird
eyes
We love of course
most
your sister has a boyfriend that
has built a cinema
layout
in the small
cottage
we sit in their sofa to
look
i look at my face
in the bathroom
afterwards
try to see if i
look like
like Liv Tyler

4.
the woods are the woods are the woods
seaks the dog

play dead to
to come to life

awaken the search
instinct

do i   *breath e*
do you   *breath e*

give candy
lick the fingers

5.
We lie close
on the leather sofa
skin meets leather
dead against life
you pound my head
in to the breasts
i want to stay
in the warm
is it summer or
only fever

6.
Your sister's boyfriend calls us
anus-kids, mini-sluts
We know yet nothing
We whisper it in the night
We are the pride glittering

7.
one day
we find

a dead
rat under

the hay in
the stables it

pulls
somewhere inside me

we bury it in
in the grit

it gets
a pile where the ground

don't want it inside it

8.
we play wild

9.
ride draw
draw horses ride pigs ride on
stools and trestles and other stuff
that one can ride on
ride the horses
draw the horses
i can do it just like
nature
it is only therefore that
you can be with me

10.
run run
over the wild
heart

11.
it comes water through the skin

12.
what would we do
if we were not

what would we do
in the loneliness
we

can't bother to hang out
you push

my elbows
against the box wall

i lick blood from
your lips

i need much
iron

13.
When you Forget

chew your own teeth

BLACK MOULD   THE SMELL   ALL THAT IS
SAFETY

Barbie : the horses _ the dreams : plexi glass

mtv : fuck head : card game : dreams

and i said i should
do everything for you like
you only do for
the one you
ARE

the clock would be eight
we had already been awake
and gone with the bus
for hundred hours

puuuuh.

Horses : Horses : Horses

bear : bind : blind : belts : belt : stuck : fight

I am this little child that just
Ooooooooooo
That just
I am this weird adult
Girl that
Grl
Carry her breasts
Nothing
Flat from
Nothing
Of the milk that flows
Mouth corners
Dry tender wit
A napkin
Glossy from powder

hearsay : hounds : hounds coming

one in the class that has : a dad : that has

lynx

in a yard : go there if you dare
look at
the cats

i would carry
the light first of all
they had picked me because i was
the chosen
who would be
chosen
to the god

Often I feel a bit
Low

LILA
PINK LILA

MANE TAIL   HOLLOW   SHOULDER BREAST
FUR

FOREHEAD

summer : night _ nights : haymow
as if . you should

lose it : HERE

I just know
Not
So much

BEAR
PINK ROSA MOUTHS LIP GLOSS MINT LIQUORICE
& RASPBERRY
STREAM

And then would the body flow away like
A little boat
The small animals would be drawn to
The corpses
Would go
Like with a ferry
They would
Sing
Karaoke
On the dead throat they would
Enjoy

Caress : carry : caress : groom : glossy

Fur : hair :

Skin

Skin

Skin
Skin
Skin

EXACTLY THAT THAT I WANTED
DID NOT WANT WANT WANT NOT JUST
BEGGING FOR IT

eat of her

_ will you now cut the baby out of the body
_ are we grown up now
_ ?????
_ i feel only for you
_ fuck u
_ do you remember that we . . .
_ barely
_ run in the hay
_ how it fell over fallen

We should talk about your illness
My illness
We should

Purple horses and the scent of gasoline

Morning
Lumps

I will talk a little with you now because

This can't go on

What do you mean when you say that
What you say that
          What you state that
It's lying
Purple wet

I will take a bath on the floor

It is the ichor from your wounds
It is me that hurt you

It is my assignment
To lick your wounds

Your genitals of
Wounds

If you wanted to let me take care of
Hand
Hands
Good soft hands

You have given it all to me
And I have taken it
As a threat
As a wound
I accidentally eat
What you give me
And I accidentally own
Nothing of it
That belongs to you

_ can we speak now as adult people
_ i don't think so
_ or will we remain children till this
_ moment
_ if i was a room you would be a time
_ i will fuck the life out of you
_ i know you don't mean it
_ i am serious
_ there is too much tenderness

MORNING
DREAM
BLOODY
KNEES
SOLES
ASSIDUOUS
WISHING TIRED
FORGIVE
PILES OF DESTINY
EVENINGS
DINNERS
LIGHT BLUE
SLEEP

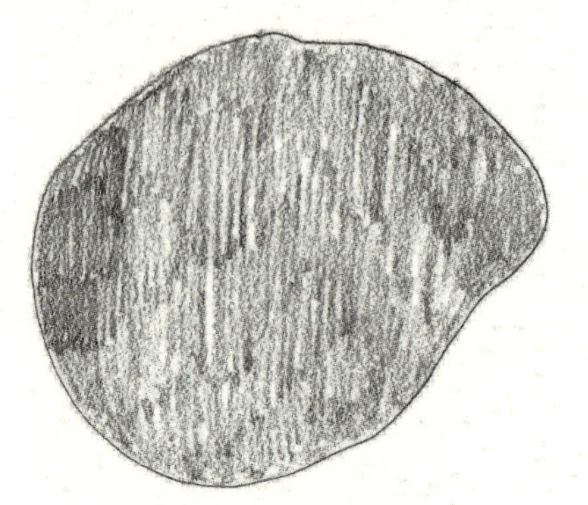

No one guards the body
            The urge to say something *else*

Soft Skin Skills Scary Sleep

We can never be as old
We can never be old
We can never grow up
I have pushed in my old
Teeth
In your shoulder
There is your blood
In my mouth
In my lips

Red
Wet

_ should we
_ sleep
_ should we lie
_ in the dark, talk
_ pretend
_ as if
_ without guilt
_ dig
_ nylon around the throat

The soul
Has not yet » arranged «

Skin as skin

Stream

think about the cat !

Here is a hand
It lies down on the leg
Cold white bones
Right inside the hip

Here is a mouth
All inside
The skin

she
she
she
a hole of her
she her sex
a kitty
a female cat
she who carries you
as her kids
the body heavy with kids
carry too heavy
the cat that runs
with the life
for life
inside
all too heavy
the spine sinks
hollows
the weight against the bones
white bones
skeleton
hip bones
hand
the bones of the cat

the young and horny

i carry their grief

with all i want and need now

cat paws

on the breasts

now she is in labour

they will fuck

life out of youth

i hate

i carry the small things

sticky fur

catcatcatcatcatcatcatcatcatcat

(mimesis)

Don't touch more

Things; Production; Criterias

tremble

hard light /

rare & bitter

Bitter flesh.

Biografy; Childhood; Landscape

street

fingers in mouth

center

rain drops

shot
shoot
sick

horse knees greetings

The birthday
Christmas eve
I should carry
I carry the burden

Powder over

Soft
Skin
Wound
Pocket in the brain
River
I flicker

Take something down to
The throat pit
Let it lie
Bury
Keep
The chairs as they are in the room
As in the room as in the light
You can see the powder
As the air
As the lungs
As the cats
As

I carry my soft fur
I am a fold
In to the heart

Numb

Heart.

R I V E R

When I am born I am blue. I disappear under the white lace of a knitted cap. All those who have come before me must nurture me as I lie inside the incubator glass. It glistens there so slowly. I let my heart sound, a quiet murmur. It will settle like a veil over Mother, she will not be able to remember without it. There will come a time when it will always be silent. There will come a time. I'm taken home to the Cat. Cat has the same colour as the floor, I'm still weird. The Cat licks weirdness with Cat's tongue. Cat wants me to be a cat so it can scratch me, so it can scream at me, so I understand, it's still a long way until we can make love. Mother is afraid of Cat doing things to me. *Mother says about Cat: RIVER. River is a word fed to my mouth now. In River there is me. The words are River. Claws scratching turns into River. Scars from scratching are River in River words tell me. Cats in River. Claws belong to cats and crows. Claws are longing for River. Later I learn. River translates. River with Mother's tongue is the act of claws scratching of clawing in skin in tree in thing. It translates. It transforms later. River is water is running crack in earth. River is scratching. River is running. Claws make River. River makes blush in crack around crack in face. River laughs.* The old Mothers walk side by side. I shake when I sleep. This body is so fragile. It breaks and grows together. I lie in a wagon that Mother pulls with these other Mothers. They will remember that we walk there together, it will bind us together forever, it's not something you can forget. They walk across the old railway. Cat claws scratch my face. Mother saying Mum saying Mummy. *Mum is worried with the river in my face. Mummy worried words the call. The name. Mum gives me Name.* ANNA. All this has been said to me. For I myself remember nothing before the Sibling. Things fall from the sky. Mother says: how she puts us under the tables. Mothers know you can't trust anyone. Anything that scrutinizes. It must be a real measure. Airplanes in the blue. Bits of my body end up in the Sibling's. My arm movement as I feel for the eyebrows: it is still there, is where the Sibling grows. I must nurture it, learn at once. The Sibling in me, me in the Sibling. The eyes outside me end up on the movement, mimicking, mimicking, don't we have eyebrows? It's like it's important. We. It scares me that it could be out there doing something untrustworthy. The Sibling always moves close to me. It doesn't want to die it wants to live. I just have to learn the tenderness. *When Anna transforms into* ANNAN. *It means with Mother's tongue Other. Later they tell me it means other. It becomes other River. River means with Mother's tongue tear. It means wreck. It means the act of grating carrots making carrots from big to small. All small carrots inside carrots. Grating cheese means River. All small cheeses inside cheese. River tells me. Words tell me River is world with claws scratching.* I put my face in Mummy's dress. I have to hide from the sun. A lump of body. I turn my face away from them. I can't stand so many. They shine from the sun. Everyone else shines so strangely. My body is drawn into me. I devour everything. I devour everything. I eat it in pieces. It fills me until I'm full. There in me it lies, pressing. I wrap my legs around my torso. I wrap my clothes around it. I hide it inside me. Inside, it grows. Soon it's all over me. It's in the blood. I'm a little shellfish under the surface of the water. An adult holds me there. I want to come up, but I can't breathe there. I'm always at parties. But you hardly notice me at all. The adults are closer than the children. I don't understand them. The children stay away. The adults laugh at me. I feel the shaking of the laughter. It feels like a body. Body and River. *Belonging to fish longing for fish hold in hands with claws and fur. Crow make scratch with claws in scar. Crow place a word and word is heart. Birdheart.* I'm just going to lie down under a bush. It's safer there. The ground is warm against my skin. It nurtures me and takes me in. It wants me to be there. All low and close. I take clay from a pit and build myself a house. A wall until the pit is empty. A wall against the world. There are sticks with thorns scraping against my arms. I pull them there, light pricks and thin scratches. I get all scared. *River tell fish. Cat Fish is a tale of 2 River. Fish pretending cat. Cat deceiving fish. Later I learn. With Mother's tongue the Cat-Fish's Name is MAL. With Other tongue MAL is bad. With Mother's tongue Bad is a Word 2 give 2 God. God's Name is almost good and good they say is the evil twin of bad they say the feeling of bad is the feeling of no-no-no-good and good translates to Mother's Word: Frisk. & Sibling later writes 2 me they hope I will be Frisk but Sibling miss-spells the Word and Frisk with Sibling's writing transforms into Fisk and Fisk is Mother's tongue's Word and it is Fish. Fish lives in River. MAL writes a Book of Flowers. Fish Flowers Floods Face.* I hear strange noises in the forest. I walk there with other adults. There are a lot of big people. And then me and the Sibling. I feel how the time is different. We'll find a little cottage here, we'll escape there when they come to hunt us. I know that soon all the adults will die out and only me and the Sibling will be left. We have to make it on our own. It's a pity that the Sibling is so bad at everything he tries to do. When the bad guys come, we'll climb out the windows and down the trellis. I have to help the Sibling even though my body is just as bad. The mud gets stuck in my legs. The fabric around it moves so slowly slowly. We run hidden. The little cottage is drawn on the cardboard. There are strips of curtains in the windows. Here you can live undisturbed. They would never look here. *The name.* I write my name backwards and forwards across the papers. Single down over the leaves. Laughter. As I sit under the table, I hear my mother say my name: *anna* sticks out of the other speech, which is hazy and blurry. She says my name many times, but I know she doesn't want me to come out and be visible, because the name sounds completely different. She says the strange name and soon they start laughing. I hear the laughter of adults and they scare me. I can't stand to hear such unfinished sounds. I can't tell if they become animals or remain something else. I lie flat on the floor. I can never be seen again. I feel it like a pit inside me that grows until I'm lying right in it. Dark earth is laid over it. There I lie until the Cat comes. I force myself to open my eyes because the Cat needs me. She needs my tenderness more than anything. I stroke her white chest where it's smoothest, then her back and neck. Around us is a forest of legs. I can't imagine that I have legs like that too. Mine are under me, folded up. I think they've been cut off at the knees. Blood splashes across the fur. I think the war is still here. The mothers will have to run up soon. It comes all of a sudden. In the middle of the party. They're coming to get us. Only I, hiding under the table, will be left behind. I'll have to do everything myself from now on. Already I can stir the pots of meat sauce. I know where the sheets are in the cupboards. Maybe the Sibling can stay too. Maybe the

Sibling and I can lie in the chrysalis and be chrysalis ourselves. Maybe, it has such soft skin. I press my chin against Sibling's forehead. Rubbing, softly, softly. Remembering Sibling's tiny little teeth as they tickle my belly button. I love it anyway. There's a rabbit living under the house, they're trying to get it out with long sticks. My fur is the same colour. I lick it clean so it shines. I can't wear panties, but no one will know. There's something about me that's all sensitive. Only dresses I can wear. My skin bleads. It stings and tears. The fabric has to be big and flying to be with me. I hide underwear behind the cushions on the sofa. The mother finds them after I forget. I get scared of all the angry people. When the mother becomes one of them, her body changes. How can this be the same. How can anyone stay the same. I feel I'm not to be trusted. Suddenly I can tear and bite or hit with something. *Face belonging to River. My face is a Catfish. Mum saying stop lying with face.* The Sibling has to do as I say or it will be the one that happens to me. It is so small and easy to torture. I'm afraid my gaze will hurt. I'm afraid of me. I have to shut myself in, so I crawl inside the duvet. My mother carries me on her shoulders, over all that is needed. I have to lie still so that no one notices that I am not a mass of wood but a piece of meat. *Cat calling me.* I miss Cat. I call Cat Oh! When Mom calls *ANNA*, I hear it again, that's the way it should sound. She calls me. I need to get through without them getting angry, I need them to be quiet, but all of a sudden the laughter comes. They marvel that I've been there all along. What was I doing there. I am so small. Such a little scoundrel. I feel it, like knives in my skin. I don't want to be this. They have such hard hands patting me. I need my mother to be alone. She asks how it is.

I tell her I'm happy. I see her smile. I say I'm tired when she asks. She never notices that I say everything that isn't. I'm fascinated that I talk like that. I've never been able to do that before. I say things that aren't true. I can't wait for my mother to look at me and ask again if it's really true. But she smiles very quietly. I always dream about my body. The only thing I can take in is spaghetti. I eat it like long worms. The worms crawl around inside me and multiply. They grow with me and I with them. I think for a long time about all this inside me. I worry but nothing can be said. Later the worms become crustaceans, crayfish, crawling inside me. There is something about this body that I cannot grasp. I hold it around me. *River has Sibling and Sibling's name is Å. The sound of Å is Oh! River river my face with ååå oh! River laughs. River later. River claws. Thread of River. Word in water.* There is something reassuring in this but I am also very scared.

FOX.

the Fox is in the Circle

the Fox is Pink now

issues of those who feel a strong connection to the may be kitsch but it captures for me some of the movement of desire longing nostalgia and serve as an essential guide on their spirit is a project of being and longing sly nature reminds us that sometimes we used to be clever as a girl within a can only remember girls to offer the world never got over my best friend and it took me a hell help you stay focused and agile when facing vividly recalls for me the image of how girls get whetting through dense forests or urban areas around horses and of how my best friend and on instinct and intuition to make quick seemingly consciously chose each also learn to trust your flows more freely once mounted more when facing Well of Loneliness teaches us the importance of substantiates the body of for their cunning with that of her first horse follow our inner her cheek against creatures with a devious nature not you any more adds an element of mystery and magic to their are of the natural order was a fascinating figure in ancient allowed to enjoy her love for walked with the steps of a fox though her inverted love is God the Fox is White now

soft fur come lickin

the Woods are running with *foxes*

the Fox mimics the Horse in a gallop and swallows

when i am born i am blue and i am ashamed of my ugliness. no one can reasonably put up with this. i disappear under the white lace of a knitted cap. all those who have come before me must nurture me must hide this ugliness as i lie inside the incubator glass. it glistens there so slowly. i let my heart sound, a quiet murmur. it will settle like a veil over my mother, she will not be able to remember without it. there will come a time when it will always be silent. there will come a Time

fly with the Fox is an *eye*

an Eye opening the Fox for the Garden

LET ME IN

the Fox whispers

the Fox have *eyes* in the Night

the Fox is inside the Horse inside the Horse's *belly*

according to witnesses the person or persons concerned may suffer from scabies the activity of organising and shaping the whole of the protection hunters have set traps their original form was intended to establish boundary lines between the : to make passages in the outermost layer of the skin to organise the settlement in the long term and lay their eggs there and lay their eggs there could also be avoided the distinction between the terms *map* and *plan* was consistent and the drawing up of a plan for an imaginary future town was called and lay their eggs there with legislation regulating the activities of and lay their eggs there a liquid drug which the Fox is a Fish

the Fox is sleeping in the Sun

the Fox is a Light

the Light is hurting&healing

the Fox is hearing the Light and the Sorrow

it must be a real measurement. airplanes in the blue. bits of my body end up in the Sibling's. my arm moves as i feel for the eyebrows : it is still there, is where the Sibling grows. i must nurture it, learn at once. at the same time. i feel this something, it must be killed and cut out. the Sibling in me, me in the Sibling. the *eyes* outside me end up on the movement, mimicking, mimicking, don't we have eyebrows ? we can't be the same. i must separate. there's a force in me that wants to center, gather, everything inside. Me. it's like it's important. We. it scares me that it could be out there doing something untrustworthy. the Sibling always moves close to me. it doesn't want to die it wants to *live*. i just have to learn the tenderness.

the Fox is knitting a Bed and a Heart and a Morning

the feet of the fox the feet of the fox

the Softness of *foxes* the Sleep of the Sound the *opening*
Sad the Softness of Sand

the Fox is eating a Pearl and a Tooth

the Fox;   puts its *eye* in the *mouth*

the Softness of Tongues;   *calling the fox running*
slowly on seas surface a small little face of a fox   . . .
Lashes

Lips *blushing* in fox-child's Hidden Shoe

Strawberries eating *foxes*

the Sun is Broken

the Fox is building a Church in the Sea

the Fox is a Peach and an Apple

the Fox is an *ice* Cream

the Fox is a barbie Pony;   a ghost Detective;   a
Trace of a *palace*;   a Paper;   a Word

the Fox is painting

i must change my *name*, it can't be like this. O's clothes act as an extension of O. other people's clothes look so mismatched by comparison. i've crossed my fingers over all my garments and fabrics. to make them feel like they belong to me. so that they will behave in a reasonable way. but the fabric doesn't seem to get it. O's clothes stretched until they become skin. it never gets disgusting like on others. when i first see O and then look at others, i feel how everything in them is skewed, i get all disgusted. i can't look anymore. they turn into lumps of flesh. they start to smell. i think something is rotten. after O, i can't be with others anymore. being around others becomes a risk. i get scared when they get close. there's a contagion on their breath. i have to hold my breath when people other than O are near. because their bodies are contagious through the air. i get dizzy and can't *move*.

the ancient city excavations in the ruined mound an experimentation of the human experience characterized by deviations from outstanding in its relationship with but is loosely linked to the visions of *words* were no longer law had started to think through the *dream* the future could feel financially free not infrequently disputes arose over how a movement's principles should the Sword is a Mirror

the Fox is carrying a Candle and one More *thing*

to place the face
of the fox   *over*
the *other* face

& also   inside & *under*
the other-face is another fox-face

& to   *cover*
the face of the fox
as a blanket

& cosy
                              the ghost of cuteness
                    the face
          the fox
                    the cuteness of ghosts
                              a fox with the fur of a fox and a fox with
the heart of a fox
                    the wildness of texts
                    the stories of
                    trees
                    the stories of the faces inside the trees
                    a fox   trespassing trees   tranquil & cute

the Fox is in the Circle

the Fox is sleeping in the Sun

drops of *fox* in the Flesh

Notes

I live with the love for miss-spellings: I work with Spells, the magic spells and rituals of witches, the magic, dark and blooming. The spelling of wor(l)ds, finding hidden things in miss-takes. The misspelling is a i-miss-u-so-much-i-put-a-spell-on-u-thing that means a leaking of loss and belonging and silent message next-the-mind. The misspelling is a miss-take that takes care in different dangerously loving different ways.

This word, this world. It is like a fold, it is covered, and the spell is written like on the inside of the fold, so only if you read all parts of the wor(l)d carefully you will find it. Visible but hidden, like you will only find it by mistake or by searching . . . seaking the paranormaltextual, annangrammatical writings of letters to letters.

/

Sometimes my name is Anna, sometimes it is not, sometimes it is the same name but different. Anna Nygren is Anna N. is AnnaN and "annan" in Swedish means "other." It is like my other name, an expansion of my name and a hidden name inside me and a hidden thing inside me that I don't know.

I am Anna, but also not, and also not only. I am Anna and another Anna, and also just other.

/

The word PINK, and also the word KISS, means PEE in Swedish. The Swedish word for the color pink is ROSA, like a rose is a rose, but it is also one of the most common name for cows, like individual cows named Rosa. There is another, maybe older, word for ROSA that is SKÄR. SKÄR also means CUT. It is like a soft cut and a blushing cut a rose a romantic thingcolorword cutting across. SKÄRKIND is the name of the village where I was born. KIND has a meaning in English yes! In Swedish KIND means CHEEK, so SKÄRKIND is like a pink cheek like blushing but also a cut, in the cheek. It is like hurting. SKÄR also means a rock in the sea, I don't know the English word, it is like a stone a thing in water it is cutting it is a rose and it is. And the sea. When I was a child I peed in bed every night for many many years and I was woken up by my parents changing sheets and I sometimes think of this when I think of bodies of water and so. On the other side of the sea closest to where I was born there is Finland and the Swedish word in Finland for PINK is simply LJUSRÖD, light red also like a red light. I love fish and all the creatures living in lakes and rivers and oceans. The flesh of salmon is PINK. I often think of this. There is also crayfish. The Swedish crayfish are of two kinds. Those living on the west coast (where I live now) become PINK when they are cooked. Those living in lakes on the east coast (where I was born) become red when cooked. The Swedish word for CRAYFISH is KRÄFTA. KRÄFTA is also the name of the star sign CANCER in Swedish. (I think it is more of a crab in English but stars refuse to know anything about species, it is also my star sign) and also an old name for the illness CANCER I often think of this eating ocean stars and tumors the thing inside like pink and so.

This is not the reason why the words are pink in the book because of blushing, but also it is.

Acknowledgments

Page 103 of "Fox" was inspired by Elspeth Probyn's essay "Girls and Girls and Girls and Horses: Queer Images of Singularity and Desire." Horses and Girls are like my Favorite Thing. I always think and feel and write about this. Reading Probyn's essay and other work was for me an almost scary peculiar moment because I recognized things I had previously thought and felt, like a ghostly strange wonderful fascinating connection. (Probyn also wrote a book named *Blush* (!), but I did not know this when writing this *Blush*.)

/

Thanks,

I want to say thank you to everyone helping me write this book (even if you did not know it, did not know about the existence of me or the book, even if you did not intend to help), I want to say thank you to all my friends, friends I know in worlds and words. I am afraid of naming and making your names into a list, because naming is both lovely and hurting. So I just say, thank you.

Anna Nygren is an autistic, queer, and neuroqueer writer, artist, and translator. They are the author of several previous Swedish-language works, including their play-experimental translation of Hannah Emerson's chapbook *You Are Helping This Great Universe Explode*. As an artist, they work primarily with textiles and are currently at work on a piece about fish, neurodivergence, hospitals, and ideas of what a Good Life is. Nygren lives in Gothenburg, Sweden, with their cat, Zlatan.

multiverse

Multiverse is a literary series devoted to different ways of languaging. It primarily emerges from the practices and creativity of neurodivergent, autistic, neuroqueer, mad, nonspeaking, and disabled cultures. The desire of Multiverse is to serially surface multiple universes of underheard language that might intersect, resonate, and aggregate toward liberatory futures. In other words, each book in the Multiverse series gestures toward a correspondence—human and more-than-human—that lovingly exceeds what is normal and normative in our society, questioning and augmenting what literary culture is, has been, and can be.

Founded as a nonprofit organization in 1980, Milkweed Editions is an independent publisher. Our mission is to identify, nurture, and publish transformative literature, and build an engaged community around it.

We are based in Bde Óta Othúŋwe (Minneapolis) in Mní Sota Makhóčhe (Minnesota), the traditional homeland of the Dakhóta and Anishinaabe (Ojibwe) people and current home to many thousands of Dakhóta, Ojibwe, and other Indigenous people, including four federally recognized Dakhóta nations and seven federally recognized Ojibwe nations.

We believe all flourishing is mutual, and we envision a future in which all can thrive. Realizing such a vision requires reflection on historical legacies and engagement with current realities. We humbly encourage readers to do the same.

milkweed.org

Milkweed Editions, an independent nonprofit literary publisher, gratefully acknowledges sustaining support from our board of directors, the McKnight Foundation, the National Endowment for the Arts, and many generous contributions from foundations, corporations, and thousands of individuals—our readers. This activity is made possible by the voters of Minnesota through a Minnesota State Arts Board Operating Support grant, thanks to a legislative appropriation from the Arts and Cultural Heritage Fund.

Interior design by Alex Guerra
Typeset in Sabon

Sabon was designed in the 1960s for a group of German printers seeking printing consistency across Monotype or Linotype hot metal typesetting machines. Sabon was modeled after sixteenth-century typefaces designed by Claude Garamond and Robert Granjon. An early use of Sabon was the Washburn College Bible, composed in thought-unit typography by designer Bradbury Thompson and featuring frontispieces by Josef Albers. Sabon was also used to print the 1979 *Book of Common Prayer* used by the Episcopal Church, as well as their secondary liturgical texts, such as the *Book of Occasional Services* and *Lesser Feasts and Fasts*.

Milkweed Editions is committed to ecological stewardship. We strive to align our operations accordingly and to reduce their environmental impact. We are a member of the Green Press Initiative, a nonprofit coalition of publishers, manufacturers, and authors working to protect the world's endangered forests and conserve natural resources. *blush / river / fox* was printed on acid-free 30% postconsumer-waste paper by Versa Press.